The Story of a Crayon

It Starts with Wax

Robin Nelson

Lerner Publications ◆ Minneapolis

Lerner Publications Company
An imprint of Lerner Publishing Group, Inc.
241 First Avenue North
Minneapolis, MN 55401 USA

For reading levels and more information, look up this title at www.lernerbooks.com.

Image credits: Gabriel Perez/Moment/Getty Images, p. 3; DEX IMAGE/Getty Images, pp. 5, 23 (wax); William Thomas Cain/Getty Images, pp. 7, 9, 13, 15, 17, 19, 23 (machine) (shaped) (worker); Kosolovskyy/iStock/Getty Images, p. 11; David Tonelson/Shutterstock.com, p. 21; JGI/Getty Images, p. 22. Cover: artisteer/iStock/Getty Images (crayons); R.Tsubin/Moment/Getty Images (crayon drawing).

Main body text set in Mikado a Medium.
Typeface provided by HVD Fonts.

Editor: Andrea Nelson **Designer:** Lauren Cooper

Library of Congress Cataloging-in-Publication Data

Names: Nelson, Robin, 1971– author.
Title: The story of a crayon : it starts with wax / Robin Nelson.
Description: Minneapolis : Lerner Publications, [2021] | Series: Step by step | Includes bibliographical references and index. | Audience: Ages 4–8. | Audience: Grades K–1. | Summary: "How does hot wax become a colorful crayon? Captivating photos and text guide readers through the process"— Provided by publisher.
Identifiers: LCCN 2019036555 (print) | LCCN 2019036556 (ebook) | ISBN 9781541597723 (library binding) | ISBN 9781728401072 (ebook)
Subjects: LCSH: Crayons—Juvenile literature. | Paraffin wax—Juvenile literature. | Manufacturing processes—Juvenile literature.
Classification: LCC TS1268 .N453 2021 (print) | LCC TS1268 (ebook) | DDC 547/.77—dc23

LC record available at https://lccn.loc.gov/2019036555
LC ebook record available at https://lccn.loc.gov/2019036556

Manufactured in the United States of America
1-47917-48363-11/22/2019

I color with crayons.

How are they made?

Wax is melted
in a factory.

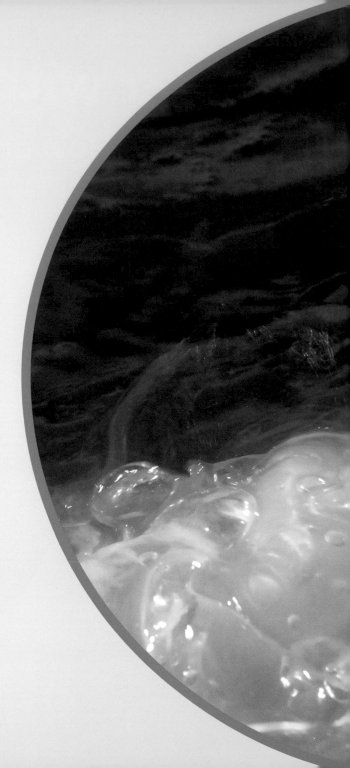

A worker adds color.

The wax is shaped.

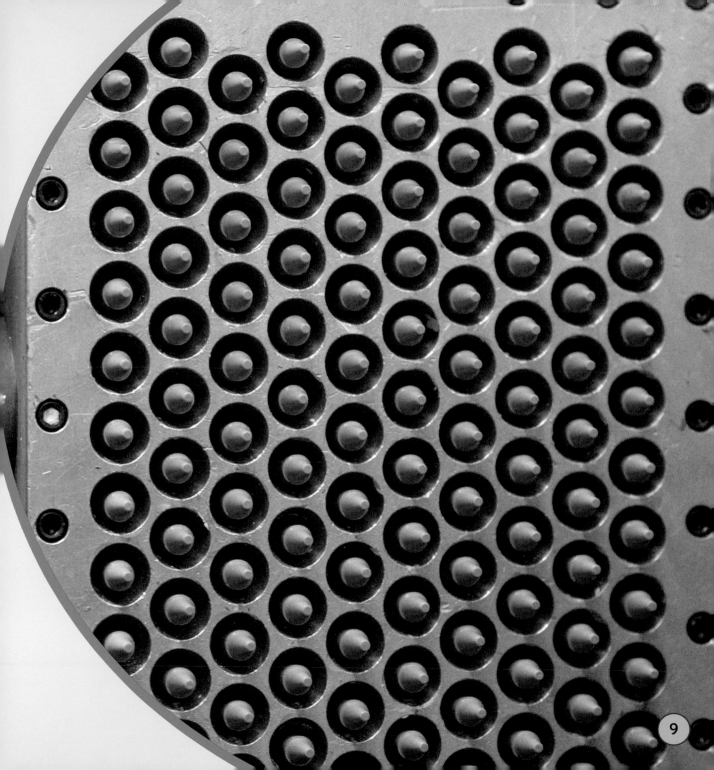

The wax gets hard.

The crayons are wrapped and put in boxes.

A worker checks the crayons.

A machine sorts
the crayons.

The crayons are packaged.

The crayons are sent to stores.

I draw pictures
with many
colors.

Picture Glossary

machine

shaped

wax

worker

Read More

Miller, Derek L. *Crayons*. New York: Cavendish Square, 2020.

Nelson, Robin. *The Story of a Baseball Bat: It Starts with Wood*. Minneapolis: Lerner Publications, 2021.

Schuh, Mari. *The Crayola Counting Book*. Minneapolis: Lerner Publications, 2018.

Index